Draw... Then Wr

Use Drawing to Motivate Writing

In *Draw…Then Write* students follow picture and written directions to draw animals, people, and vehicles. The finished drawings provide motivation for creative writing.

Writing: Jo Ellen Moore
Joy Evans
Content Editing: Marilyn Evans
Art Direction: Cheryl Puckett
Cover Design: Cheryl Puckett
Illustration: Jo Larsen
Design/Production: Jo Larsen

EMC 731

Evan-Moor®
EDUCATIONAL PUBLISHERS
Helping Children Learn since 1979

Congratulations on your purchase of some of the finest teaching materials in the world.

For information about other Evan-Moor products, call 1-800-777-4362, fax 1-800-777-4332, or visit our Web site, www.evan-moor.com. Entire contents © 1999 EVAN-MOOR CORP. 18 Lower Ragsdale Drive, Monterey, CA 93940-5746. Printed in USA.

How to Use Draw...Then Write

The 30 topics in this book are presented in three levels of difficulty, allowing you to customize the lessons to the needs of your students. You may want students to progress through all three lessons on a topic or do only the lesson that is most appropriate.

After students have had some experience with the lessons, the reproducible pages are ideal for writing center activities.

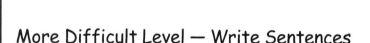

Easiest Level — Complete Sentences

Students follow three steps to complete a drawing. You may wish to guide these steps by using an overhead transparency of the page or by illustrating the steps on the chalkboard.

Students then select words from a word box to complete three sentences about the object drawn.

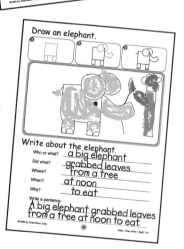

More Difficult Level — Write Sentences

Students follow three steps to complete a drawing. Next, students write phrases to answer who, what, where, when, and why questions about the drawing. Finally, students use the phrases to write an interesting sentence about the drawing. (You may want to brainstorm as a class and write the phrases on a chart before beginning the activity.)

Most Difficult Level — Write Paragraphs

Students are challenged to draw the object in a new situation. They then write a paragraph about the picture, following the writing prompt provided. Capable writers can extend this paragraph to create an original story.

Contents

Caterpillar 4

✓Bird 7

✓Mouse 10

Turtle 13

Snail 16

Frog 19

Elephant 22

Puppy 25

Lion 28

Pickup Truck 31

Koala 34

Robot 37

Clown 40

Helicopter 43

Duck 46

Hippo 49

Race Car 52

Shark 55

Rabbit 58

✓Bear 61

Porcupine 64

Monkey 67

Cat 70

Fox 73

Octopus 76

Fish 79

Airplane 82

Dragon 85

Child 88

Castle 91

Whale 94

Draw and write.

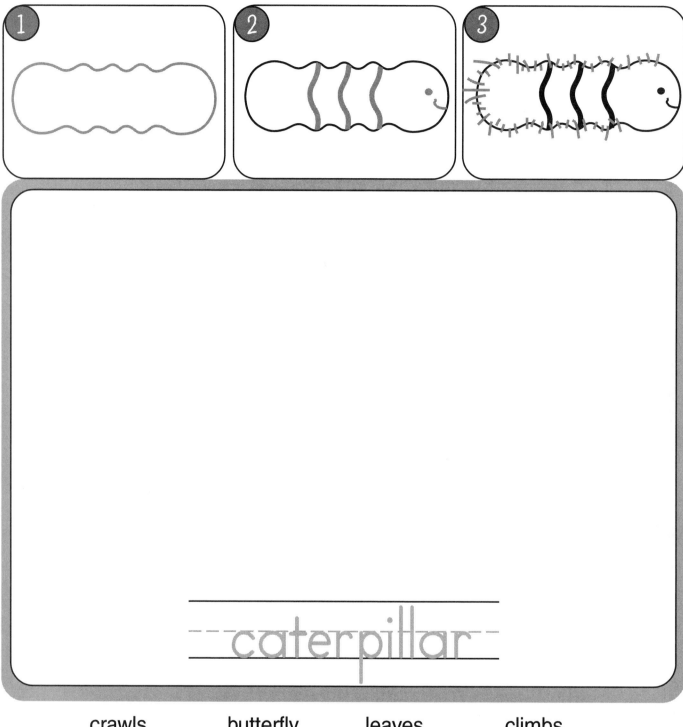

crawls   butterfly   leaves   climbs

walks   flowers   plants   moth

A caterpillar _____on little feet.

A caterpillar eats _____.

Someday it will be a _____.

Draw a caterpillar.

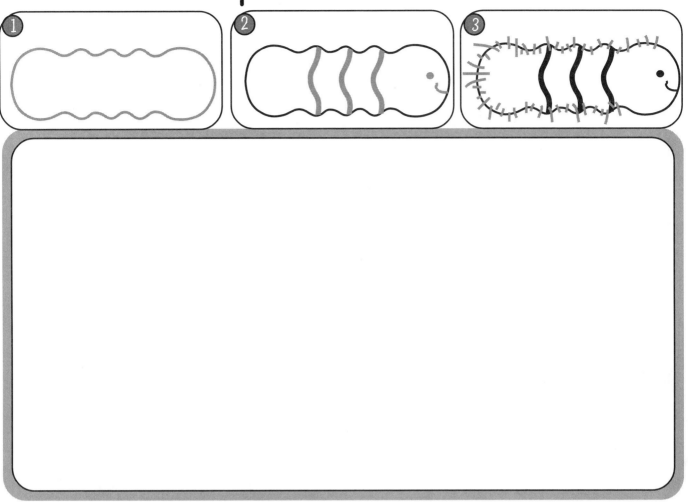

Write about the caterpillar.

Who or what? _____

Did what? _____

Where? _____

When? _____

Why? _____

Write a sentence.

_____

_____

Draw...Then Write • EMC 731

Draw

Draw a big purple caterpillar on a green leaf.

Write

Write about what the caterpillar is going to do.

_____

_____

_____

_____

_____

Draw and write.

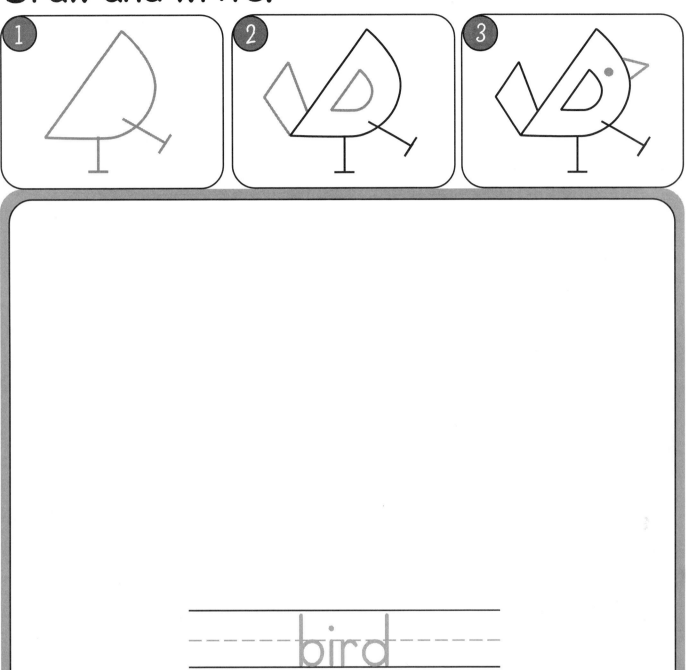

feathers   beaks   bugs   seeds

wings   nest   worms   egg

All birds have _____.

This bird likes to eat _____.

The bird will build a _____.

          Draw...Then Write • EMC 731

Draw a bird.

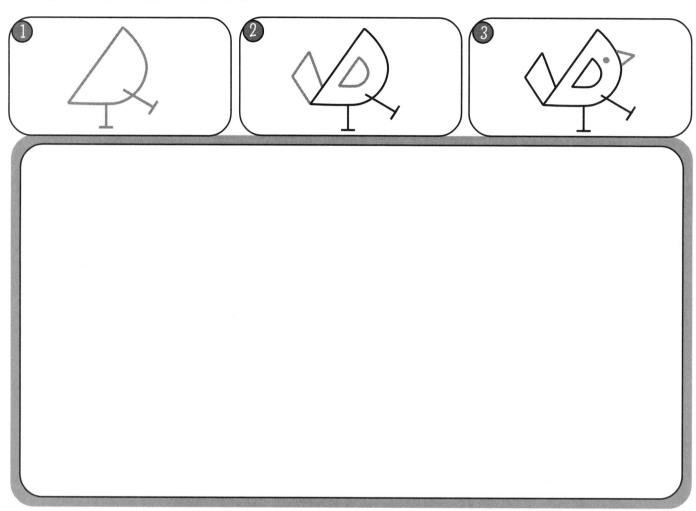

Write about the bird.

Who or what? _____

Did what? _____

Where? _____

When? _____

Why? _____

Write a sentence.

_____

_____

Draw

Draw a bird building a nest on a tree branch.

Write

Explain why the bird is building a nest.

_____

_____

_____

_____

_____

Draw and write.

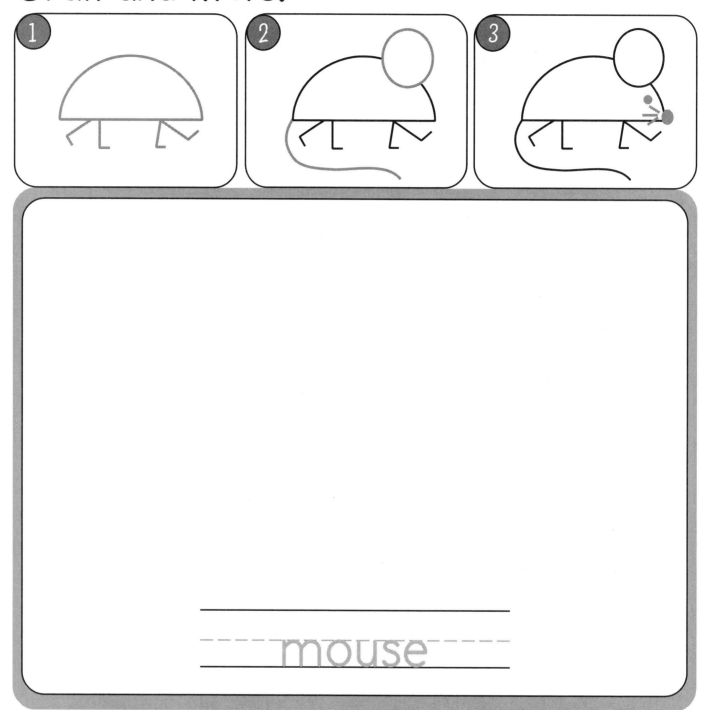

mouse

| whiskers | ears | run | seeds |
| tail | hide | cheese | jump |

A mouse has _____ and _____.

A mouse likes to eat _____.

A mouse can _____ and _____.

 Draw...Then Write • EMC 731

Draw a mouse.

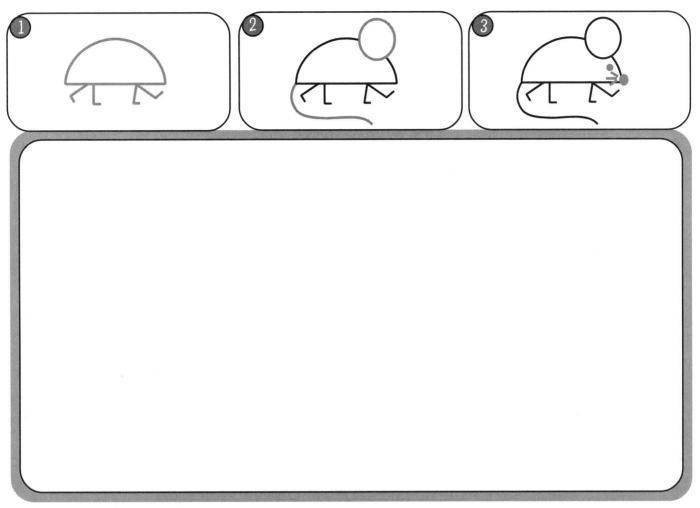

Write about the mouse.

Who or what? _____

Did what? _____

Where? _____

When? _____

Why? _____

Write a sentence.

_____

_____

Draw

Draw a brown mouse with its dinner.

Write

Write about what the mouse ate and how it got its dinner.

_____

_____

_____

_____

_____

_____

Draw and write.

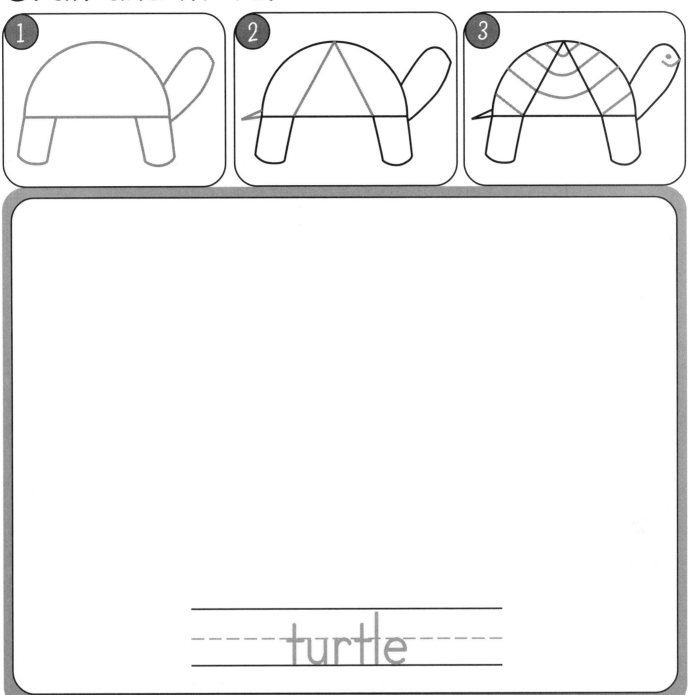

1

2

3

turtle

hard   slow   hides   green

shell   plants   fruit   brown

The turtle has a _____ on its back.

A turtle likes to nibble on _____.

A turtle moves so _____.

Draw a turtle

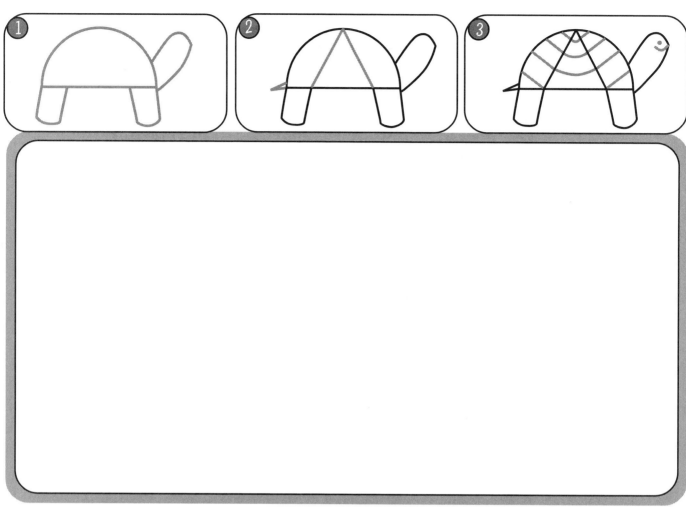

Write about a turtle.

Who or what? _____

Did what? _____

Where? _____

When? _____

Why? _____

Write a sentence.

_____

_____

Draw...Then Write • EMC 731

Draw

Draw the turtle hiding in its shell under a bush.

Write

Explain why the turtle is hiding.

_____

_____

_____

_____

_____

Draw and write.

| shell | crawls | garden | yard |
| foot | slimy | trail | plant |

A snail lives in my _____.

The snail has one _____.

It moves along on a _____ _____.

Draw a snail.

Write about the snail.

Who or what? _____

Did what? _____

Where? _____

When? _____

Why? _____

Write a sentence.

_____

_____

Draw

Draw three snails eating leaves and flowers in the garden.

Write

Describe how a snail moves.

_____

_____

_____

_____

_____

Draw and write.

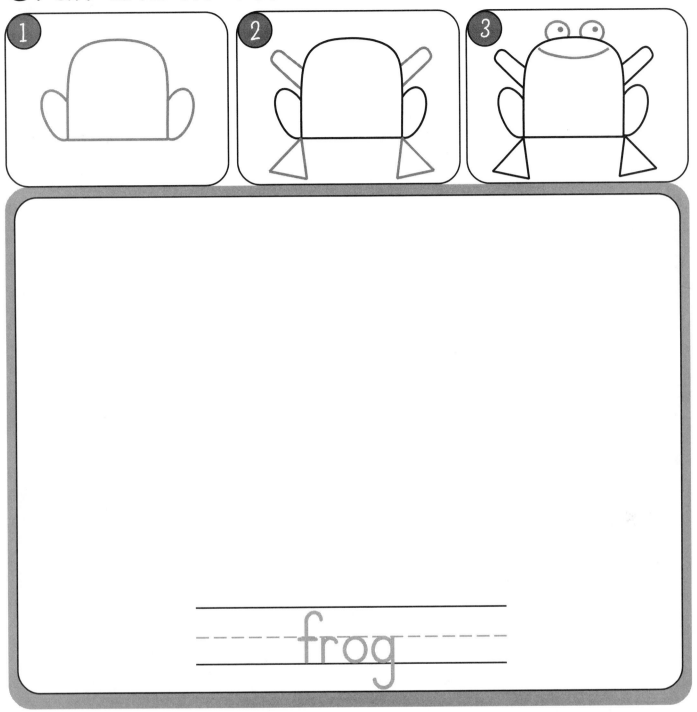

frog

eyes	pond	river	flies
feet	water	bugs	insects

The frog lives by the _____.

A frog watches for food with its big _____.

The frog catches _____ on its tongue.

Draw a frog.

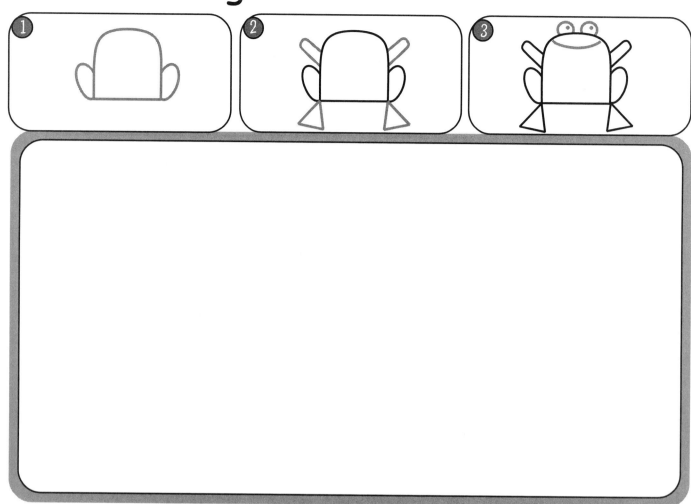

Write about the frog.

Who or what? _____

Did what? _____

Where? _____

When? _____

Why? _____

Write a sentence.

_____

_____

Draw...Then Write • EMC 731

Draw

Draw a big frog and a little frog on a log in a pond.

Write

Describe how the frogs catch their food.

_____

_____

_____

_____

_____

Draw...Then Write • EMC 731

Draw and write.

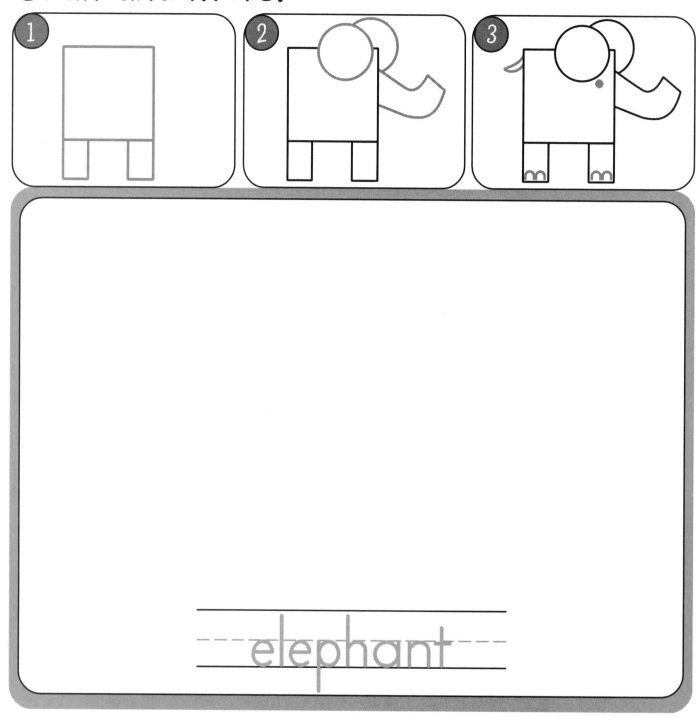

1

2

3

elephant

ears	wrinkled	leaves	water
tail	trunk	head	gray

An elephant has _____ skin.

An elephant wags its _____ back and forth.

It sucks _____ up in its trunk.

Draw...Then Write • EMC 731

Draw an elephant.

Write about the elephant.

Who or what? _____

Did what? _____

Where? _____

When? _____

Why? _____

Write a sentence.

_____

_____

Draw

Draw a baby elephant holding its mother's tail with its trunk.

Write

Write about the ways an elephant uses its trunk.

_____

_____

_____

_____

_____

Draw and write.

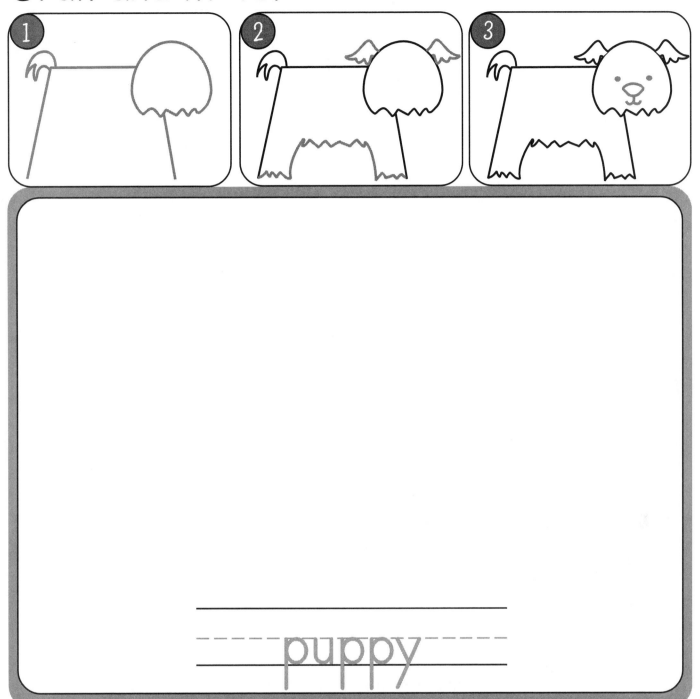

	digs	chews	bone	toy
	runs	barks	ball	bath

This puppy _____ and _____.

It wants a _____.

Sometimes it _____ holes in the yard.

Draw...Then Write • EMC 731

Draw a puppy.

Write about the puppy.

Who or what? _____

Did what? _____

Where? _____

When? _____

Why? _____

Write a sentence.

_____

_____

   Draw...Then Write • EMC 731

Draw

Draw a puppy playing in the backyard.

Write

Write about what a puppy might do.

_____

_____

_____

_____

_____

 Draw...Then Write • EMC 731

Draw and write.

hunter   wild   pounces   jumps

mane   claws   teeth   roar

A lion is a _____ .

It has sharp _____ and _____.

The lion _____ on its prey.

Draw a lion.

Write about the lion.

Who or what? _____

Did what? _____

Where? _____

When? _____

Why? _____

Write a sentence.

_____

_____

     Draw...Then Write • EMC 731

Draw

Draw a lion hiding in tall, dry grass.

Write

Write about what the lion is going to do.

_____

_____

_____

_____

_____

     Draw...Then Write • EMC 731

Draw and write.

1 2 3

_____

pickup truck

| cab | carry | cattle | feed |
| truck bed | haul | equipment | animals |

The driver sits in the _____ of the pickup.

The driver can _____ things in the back of the pickup.

The driver can carry _____.

31 Draw...Then Write • EMC 731

Draw a pickup truck.

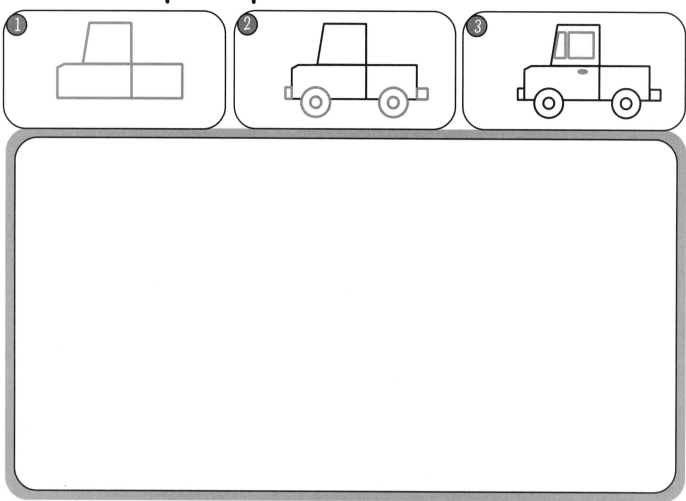

Write about the pickup truck.

Who or what? _____

Did what? _____

Where? _____

When? _____

Why? _____

Write a sentence.

_____

_____

Draw

Draw a pickup carrying a large load.

Write

Describe what the pickup is carrying and where the load is being taken.

_____

_____

_____

_____

_____

Draw and write.

| gray | sleeps | chews | carries |
| furry | climbs | leaves | baby |

A koala is a _____ animal.

The koala _____ among the branches.

It _____.

Draw...Then Write • EMC 731

Draw a koala.

Write about the koala.

Who or what? _____

Did what? _____

Where? _____

When? _____

Why? _____

Write a sentence.

_____

_____

Draw

Draw a koala and its baby climbing a tree.

Write

Write about what the koala will do in the tree.

_____

_____

_____

_____

_____

Draw and write.

machine	help	metal	talk
toy	move	work	plastic

My robot is a _____.

It is made of _____.

It can _____.

Draw...Then Write • EMC 731

Draw a robot.

Write about the robot.

Who or what? _____

Did what? _____

Where? _____

When? _____

Why? _____

Write a sentence.

_____

_____

Draw

Draw a robot at work.

Write

Describe what your robot can do.

_____

_____

_____

_____

_____

Draw and write.

clown

funny	laugh	grin	flip
stumbles	giggle	jumps	tricks

A clown is _____.

A clown does _____.

A clown makes people _____.

Draw a clown.

Write about the clown.

Who or what? _____

Did what? _____

Where? _____

When? _____

Why? _____

Write a sentence.

_____

_____

41

Draw...Then Write • EMC 731

Draw

Draw a funny clown.

Write about how the clown makes people laugh.

Write

Write about how the clown makes people laugh.

Draw and write.

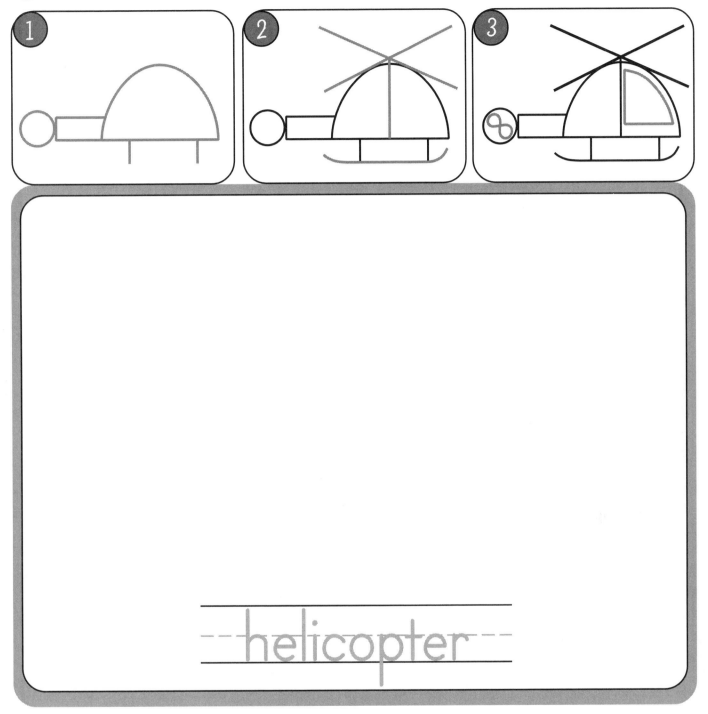

helicopter

person   propellers   fly   noise
pilot   land   loud   turn

A _____ flies a helicopter.

The _____ go around and around.

They make _____ when they _____.

43   Draw...Then Write • EMC 731

Draw a helicopter.

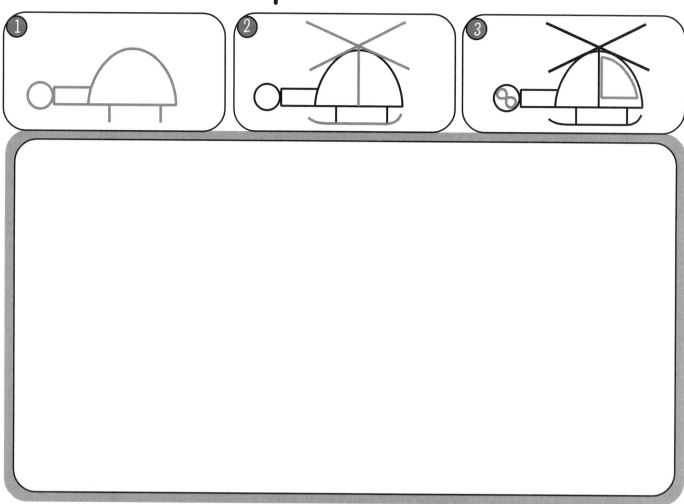

Write about the helicopter.

Who or what? _____

Did what? _____

Where? _____

When? _____

Why? _____

Write a sentence.

_____

_____

44

Draw

Draw a helicopter flying in the sky.

Write

Pretend you are the pilot. Where would you fly the helicopter?

_____

_____

_____

_____

_____

Draw and write.

duck

pond	feathers	feet	swim
water	wings	dive	fly

The duck is in the _____.

It has _____.

A duck can _____.

Draw a duck.

Write about the duck.

Who or what? _____

Did what? _____

Where? _____

When? _____

Why? _____

Write a sentence.

_____

_____

Draw...Then Write • EMC 731

Draw

Draw a duck and three ducklings in a row.

Write

Write about what the ducks are doing.

_____

_____

_____

_____

_____

Draw and write.

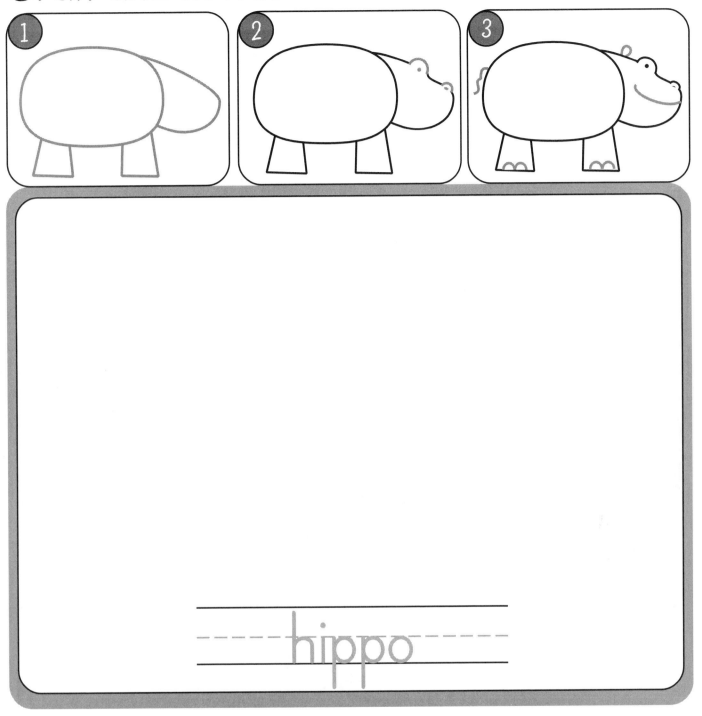

big	gray	river	water
large	smooth	grass	swim

A hippo is _____.

A hippo stays in the _____ all day.

It comes on land to eat _____ at night.

Draw...Then Write • EMC 731

Draw a hippo.

Write about the hippo.

Who or what? _____

Did what? _____

Where? _____

When? _____

Why? _____

Write a sentence.

_____

_____

 Draw...Then Write • EMC 731

Draw

Draw a hippo.

Write

Describe what the hippo is doing.

_____

_____

_____

_____

_____

51

Draw and write.

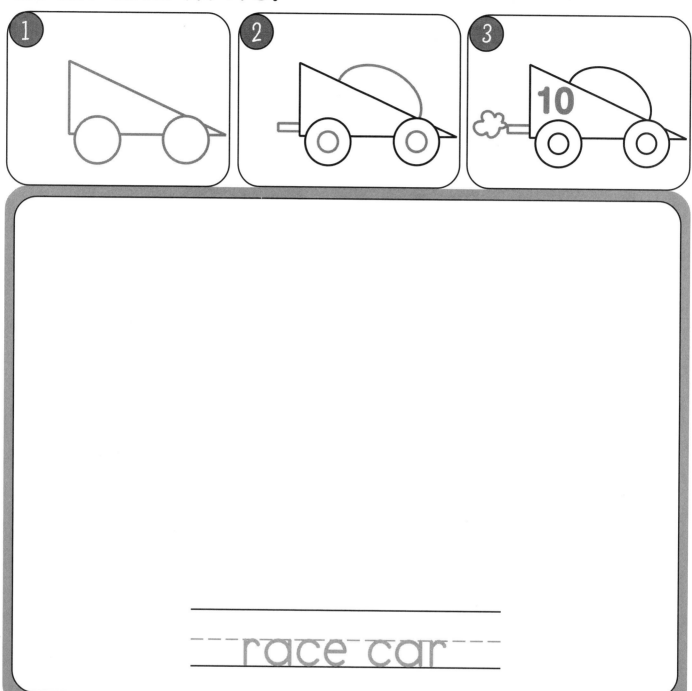

```
1
```
```
2
```
```
3

10
```

_____

race car

| races | driver | prize | quicker |
| faster | speeds | trophy | racer |

A race car _____ around the track.

The winning car goes _____ than the other cars.

The winning _____ gets a _____.

     Draw...Then Write • EMC 731

Draw a race car.

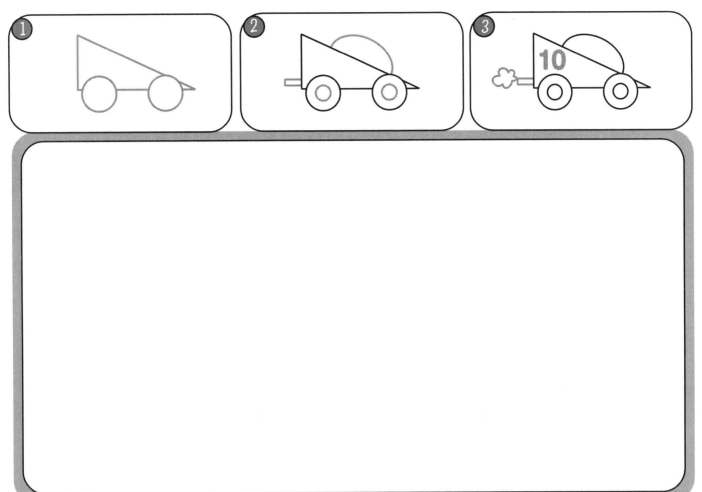

Write about the race car.

Who or what?   _____

Did what?   _____

Where?   _____

When?   _____

Why?   _____

Write a sentence.

_____

_____

Draw

Draw a race car speeding past another car.

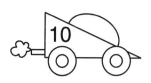

Write

Describe the race.

_____

_____

_____

_____

_____

Draw and write.

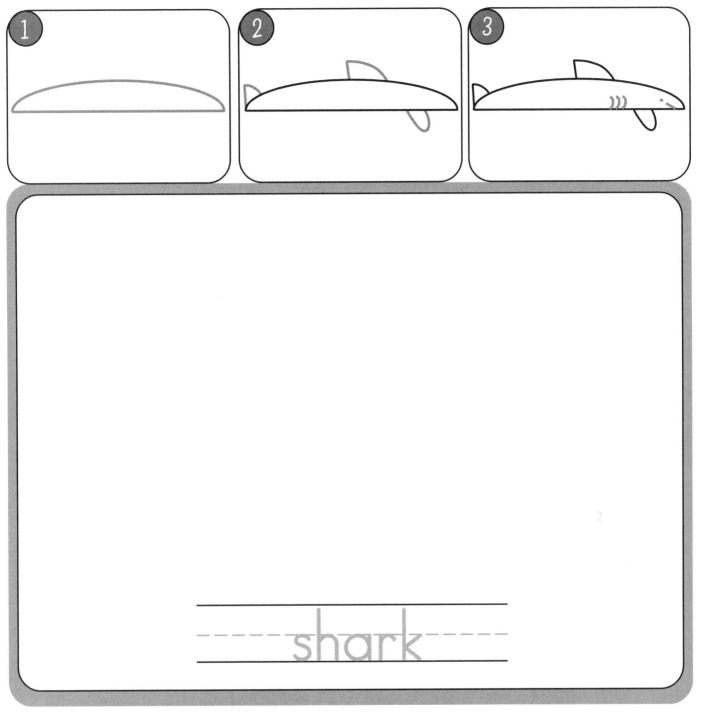

1
2
3

shark

| teeth | ocean | hunt | fish |
| fins | sea | swim | water |

A shark is a kind of _____.

A shark lives in the _____.

It has sharp _____ to help it catch food.

Draw a shark.

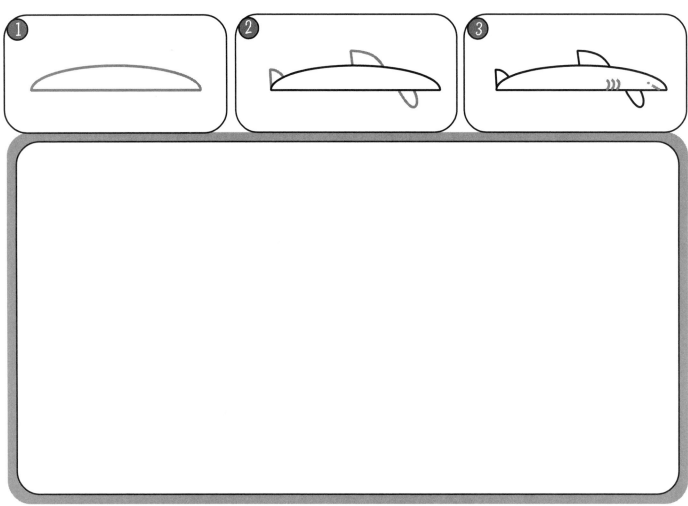

Write about the shark.

Who or what? _____

Did what? _____

Where? _____

When? _____

Why? _____

Write a sentence.

_____

_____

Draw

Draw a large shark chasing a school of fish.

Write

Write about what will happen if the shark catches the fish.

_____

_____

_____

_____

_____

Draw and write.

whiskers   wiggle   tail   jumps

furry   ears   hops   moves

A bunny has long _____ and a fluffy _____.

A bunny can _____ its nose.

It _____ on strong legs.

 Draw...Then Write • EMC 731

Draw a bunny.

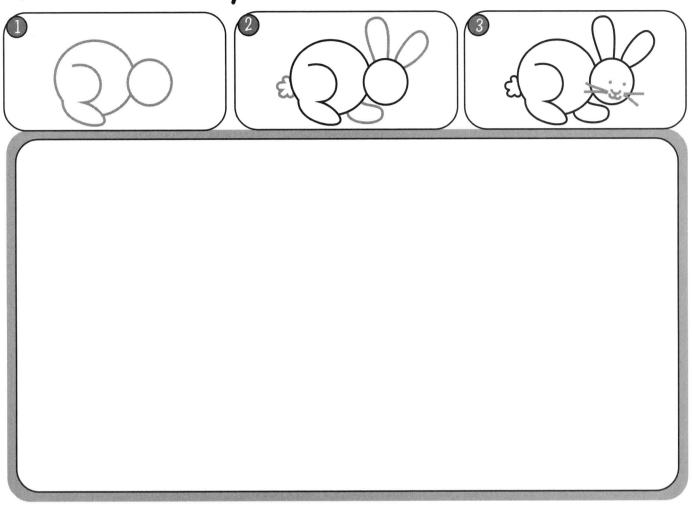

Write about the bunny.

Who or what? _____

Did what? _____

Where? _____

When? _____

Why? _____

Write a sentence.

_____

_____

Draw

Draw a brown bunny hopping across green grass.

Write

Pretend your friend has never seen a bunny. Describe what a bunny looks like.

_____

_____

_____

_____

_____

Draw and write.

```
_____

------bear------------
_____
```

| large | wild | hunts | hibernates |
| strong | furry | fishes | sleeps |

A bear is a _____ animal.

A bear _____ and _____ for food.

It _____ in the winter.

     Draw...Then Write • EMC 731

Draw bear.

Write about the bear.

Who or what? _____

Did what? _____

Where? _____

When? _____

Why? _____

Write a sentence.

_____

_____

Draw

Draw a bear by a river full of fish.

Write

Write about how the bear is going to get dinner.

_____

_____

_____

_____

_____

Draw and write.

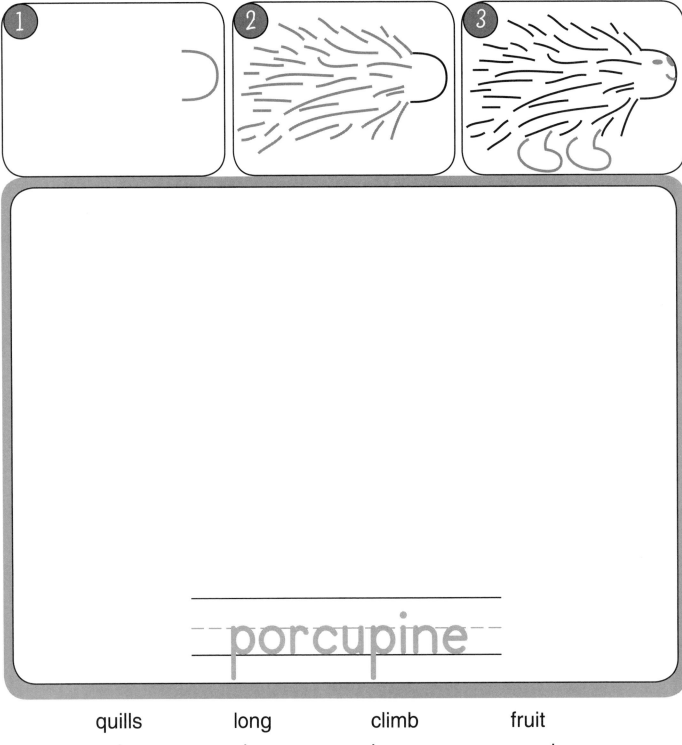

quills   long   climb   fruit

spines   sharp   leaves   seeds

A porcupine has _____.

Some porcupines _____ trees to find their food.

Porcupines eat _____.

Draw a porcupine.

①

②

③

Write about the porcupine.

Who or what? _____

Did what? _____

Where? _____

When? _____

Why? _____

Write a sentence.

_____

_____

Draw

Draw a porcupine and a dog. Show what the dog looks like after it touches the porcupine with its paw.

Write

Write about what is happening in your picture.

_____

_____

_____

_____

_____

Draw and write.

tail	climb	swing	jungle
hands	feet	jump	zoo

This monkey lives in the _____.

It uses its _____ and _____ to move in trees.

A monkey can _____.

Draw a monkey.

Write about the monkey.

Who or what? _____

Did what? _____

Where? _____

When? _____

Why? _____

Write a sentence.

_____

_____

Draw...Then Write • EMC 731

Draw

Draw a monkey in a tree.

Write

Write about what the monkey is doing.

_____

_____

_____

_____

_____

Draw and write.

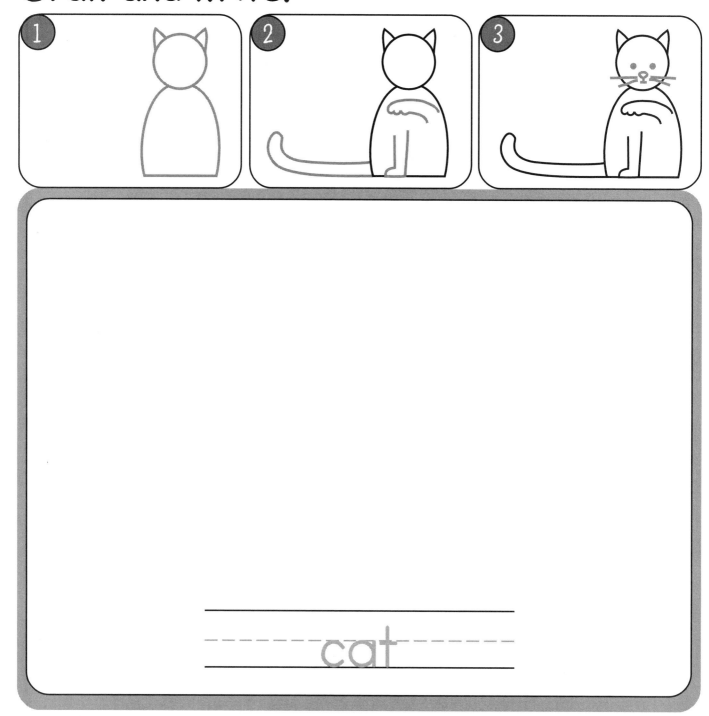

small	play	purrs	soft
furry	climb	run	pounce

A cat is a _____ animal.

It can _____.

A cat _____ when it is happy.

 Draw...Then Write • EMC 731

Draw a cat.

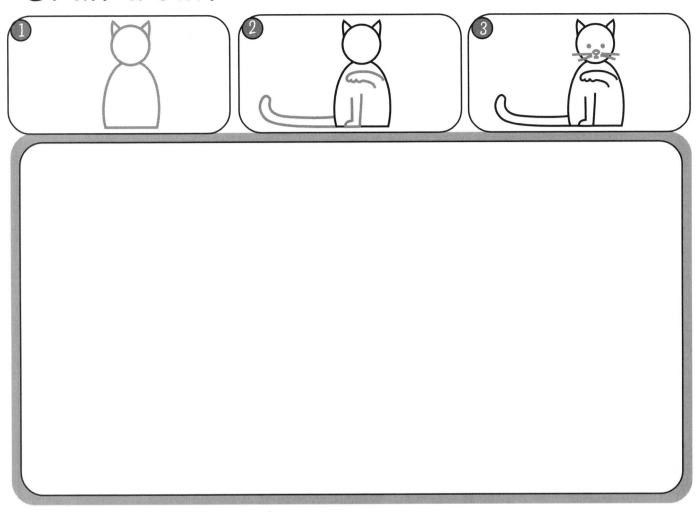

Write about the cat.

Who or what?   _____

Did what?   _____

Where?   _____

When?   _____

Why?   _____

Write a sentence.

_____

_____

Draw

Draw a cat chasing a butterfly.

Write

Write about how the cat moves as it tries to catch the butterfly.

_____

_____

_____

_____

_____

Draw and write.

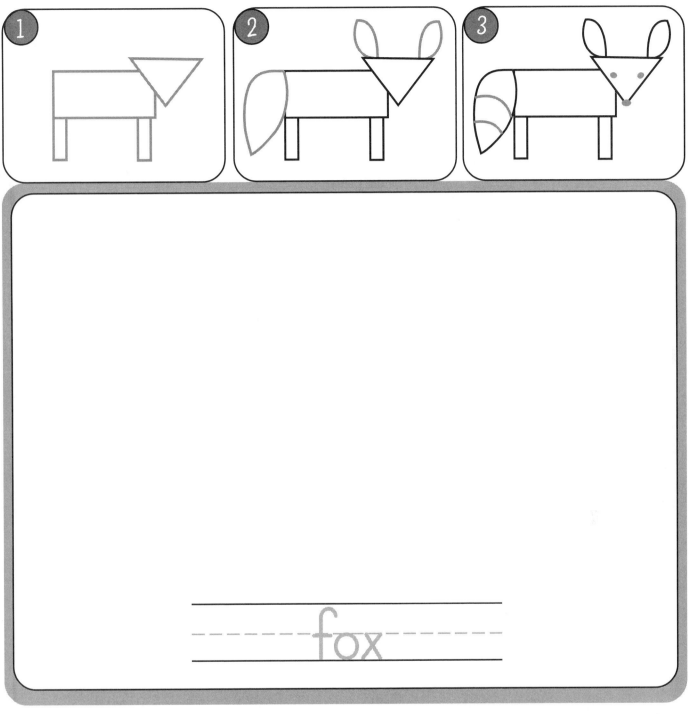

fox

| tail | hunts | den | eats |
| ears | catches | hole | bushy |

This fox has a long _____ and big _____.

It _____ small animals for food.

It lives in a _____ in the ground.

Draw...Then Write • EMC 731

Draw a fox.

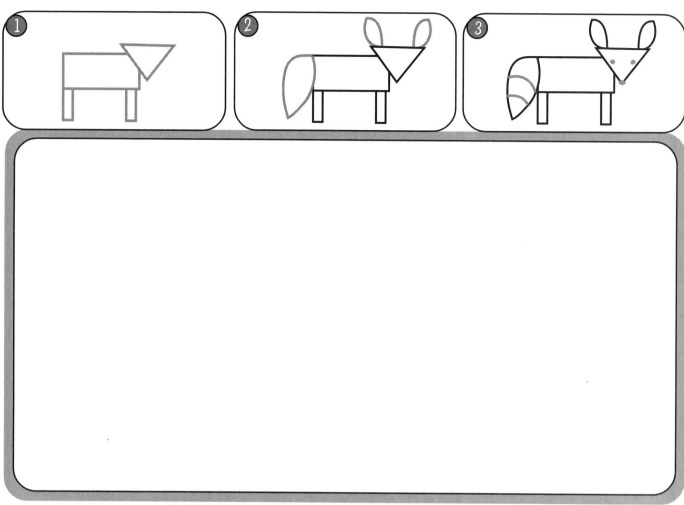

Write about the fox.

Who or what? _____

Did what? _____

Where? _____

When? _____

Why? _____

Write a sentence.

_____

_____

Draw...Then Write • EMC 731

Draw

Draw a fox in the woods.

Write

Write about where the fox is going.

_____

_____

_____

_____

_____

Draw and write.

soft   arms   ocean   rocks

colors   tentacles   sea   water

An octopus lives in the _____.

It has a _____ body with eight _____.

An octopus can change _____.

Draw an octopus.

Write about the octopus.

Who or what? _____

Did what? _____

Where? _____

When? _____

Why? _____

Write a sentence.

_____

_____

Draw...Then Write • EMC 731

Draw

Draw an octopus hiding in the rocks. Draw yourself swimming near the octopus.

Write

Write about what you would do if you met an octopus while you were swimming.

_____

_____

_____

_____

_____

_____

Draw and write.

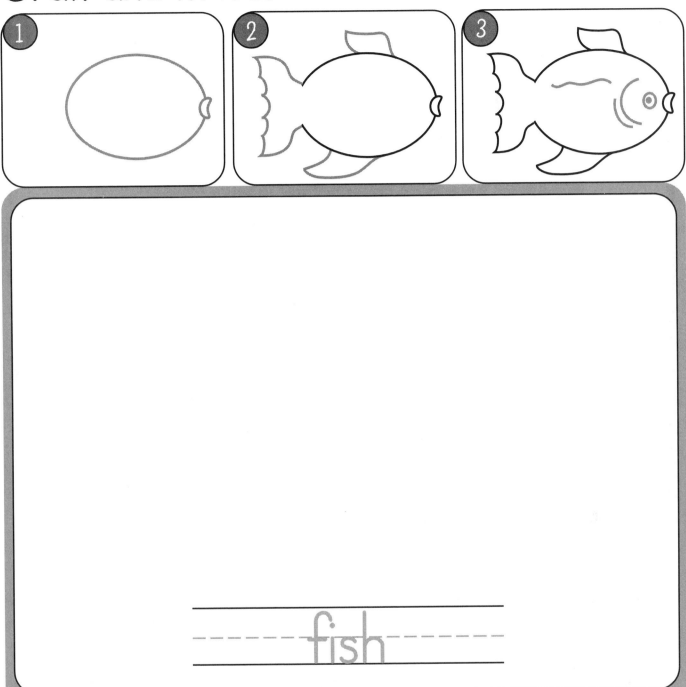

scales   tiny   tank   pet

fins   fishbowl   aquarium   gold

This is my _____ fish.

It has _____ and _____.

It lives in the _____.

Draw a fish.

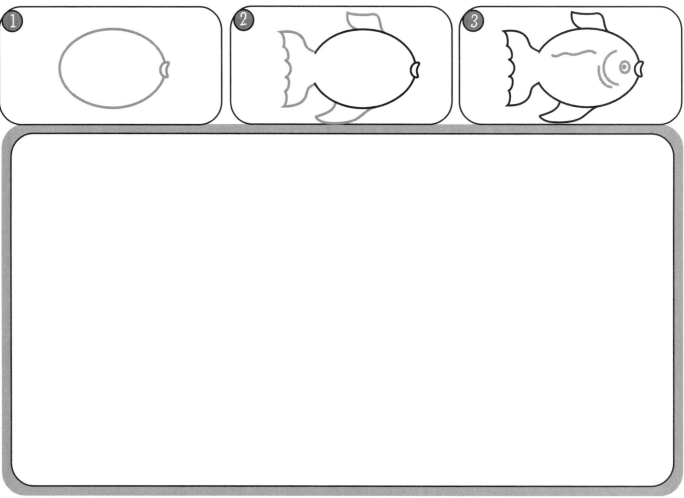

Write about the fish.

Who or what? _____

Did what? _____

Where? _____

When? _____

Why? _____

Write a sentence.

_____

_____

Draw

Draw two different fish in a large fishbowl. Add water, plants, and a snail.

Write

Write about ways that the fish are the same.

_____

_____

_____

_____

_____

Draw...Then Write • EMC 731

Draw and write.

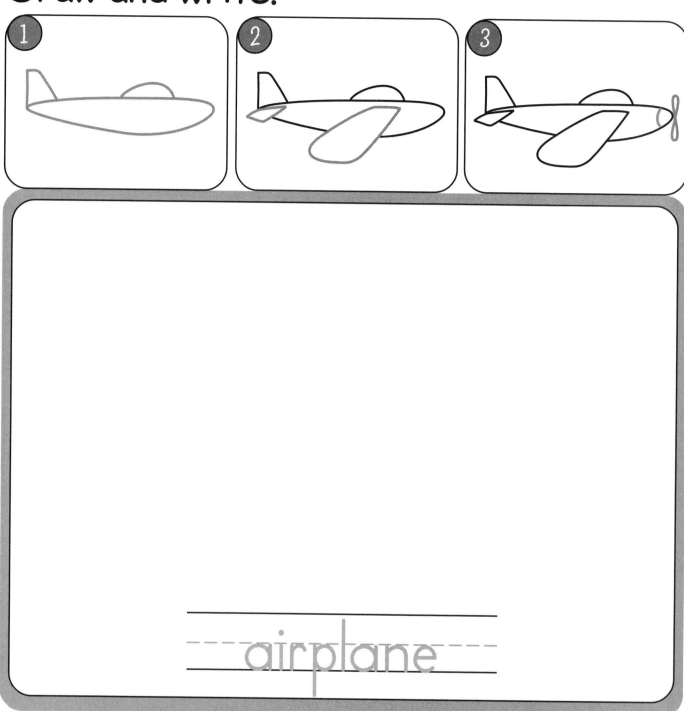

1   2   3

airplane

pilot	people	journey	engines
passengers	travelers	trip	flight

The airplane is ready to start a _____.

Many _____ get on the plane.

The _____ starts the _____ and off they go.

Draw...Then Write • EMC 731

Draw an airplane.

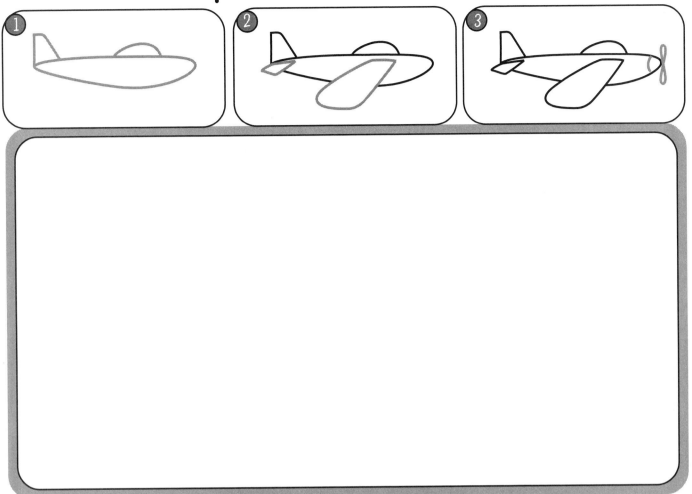

Write about the airplane.

Who or what? _____

Did what? _____

Where? _____

When? _____

Why? _____

Write a sentence.

_____

_____

     Draw...Then Write • EMC 731

Draw

Draw the airplane flying among clouds.

Write

Write about where you would like to travel on an airplane.

_____

_____

_____

_____

_____

Draw and write.

| scales | dangerous | fire | fly |
| wings | friendly | tail | scary |

A dragon has _____ and _____.

This dragon is _____.

It can breathe _____.

Draw a dragon.

Write about the dragon.

Who or what? _____

Did what? _____

Where? _____

When? _____

Why? _____

Write a sentence.

_____

_____

 Draw...Then Write • EMC 731

Draw

Draw a fierce dragon breathing fire.

Write

Write about what you would do if you met a dragon.

_____

_____

_____

_____

_____

Draw...Then Write • EMC 731

Draw and write.

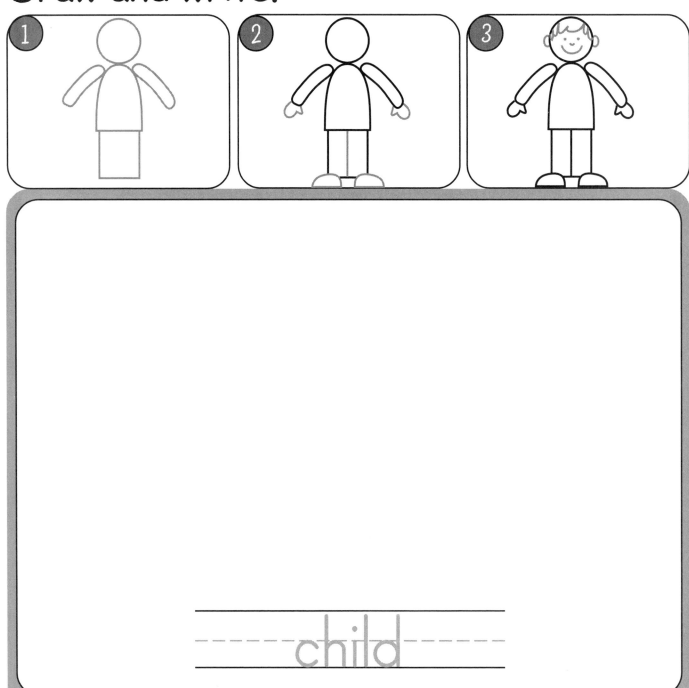

| boy | ittle | funny | sing | play |
| girl | big | smart | dance | learn |

This child is a _____.

He is _____ and _____.

He can _____.

Draw a child.

Write about the child.

Who or what? _____

Did what? _____

Where? _____

When? _____

Why? _____

Write a sentence.

_____

_____

 Draw...Then Write • EMC 731

Draw

Draw a child that looks like you. Have the child doing what you like to do.

Write

Write about what you like to do.

_____

_____

_____

_____

_____

Draw and write.

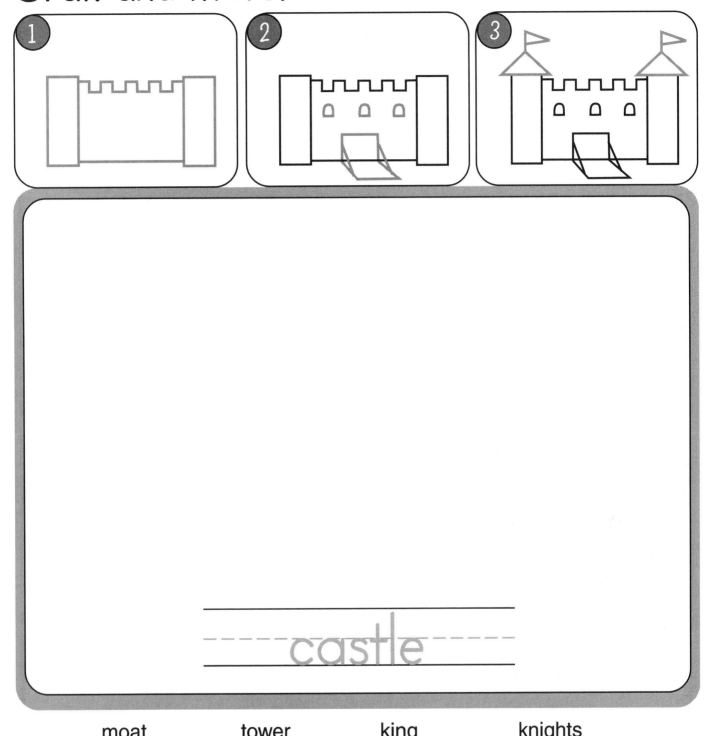

| moat | tower | king | knights |
| bridge | queen | soldiers | servants |

This castle has a _____ and a _____.

A _____ and a _____ live here.

There are _____ to protect the castle.

Draw a castle.

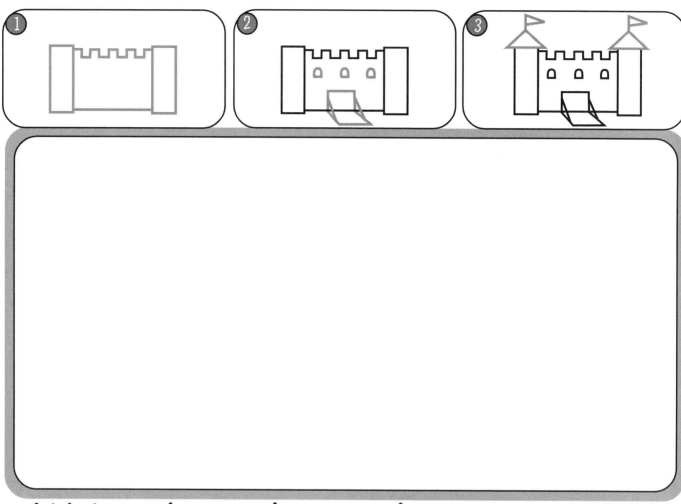

Write about the castle.

Who or what? _____

Did what? _____

Where? _____

When? _____

Why? _____

Write a sentence.

_____

_____

Draw

Draw a castle. Show the king and queen going into the castle.

Write

Write about what you think it would be like to live in a castle.

_____

_____

_____

_____

_____

Draw and write.

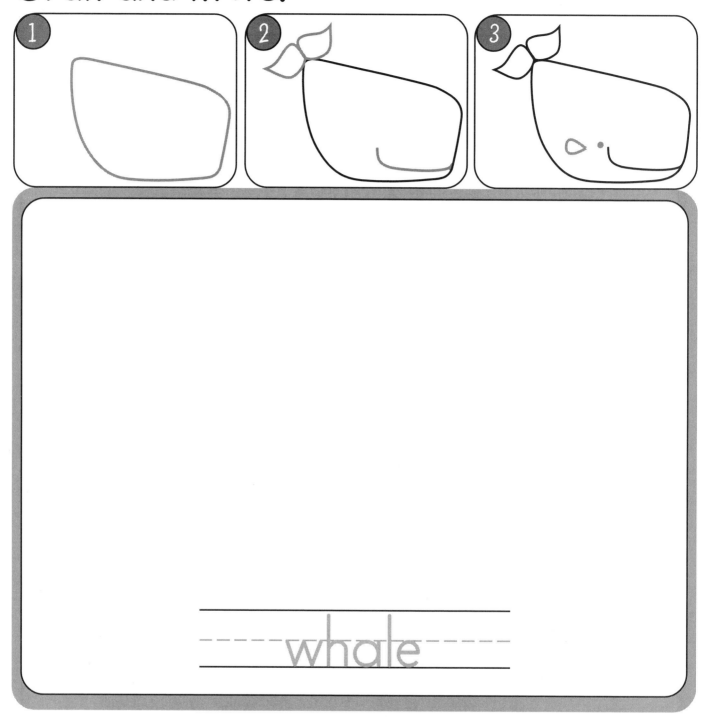

whale

| flukes | swims | ocean | air |
| flippers | dives | water | oxygen |

A whale has _____ and _____.

A whale comes out of the water to get _____.

A whale _____ in the _____.

Draw a whale.

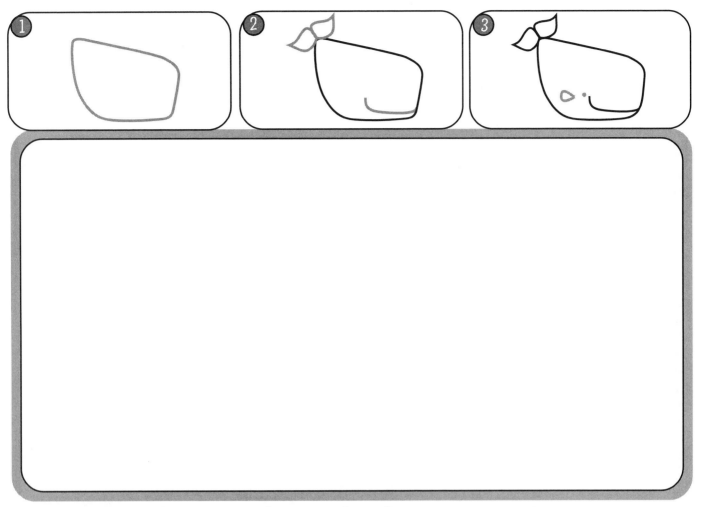

Write about the whale.

Who or what? _____

Did what? _____

Where? _____

When? _____

Why? _____

Write a sentence.

_____

_____

Draw

Draw a whale swimming along in the ocean.

Write

Write about what a whale can do.

_____

_____

_____

_____

_____

 Draw...Then Write • EMC 731